Trucks on the road. They work hard.

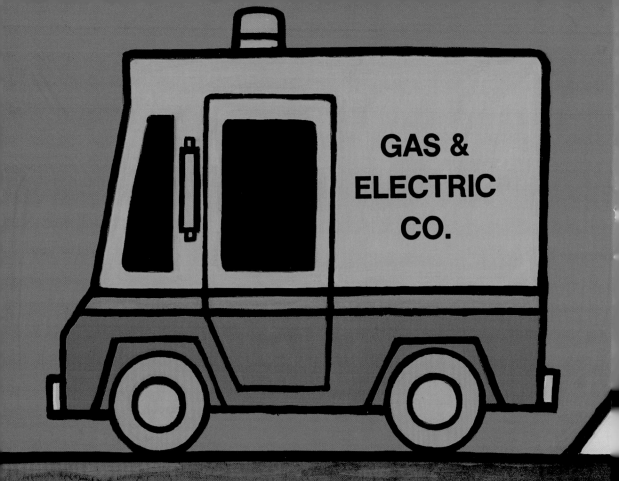

GAS &
ELECTRIC
CO.

Here is a truck working all night long.

mixing cement.

This is a cement truck

hauling dirt.

Here is a dump truck

and ice cream and soda.

This truck brings hot dogs

bringing the furniture.

Here is a moving truck

Here comes a tow truck towing a car.

delivering oil.

This is a tank truck

to help fix the lights.

Here is a bucket truck

bringing the newspapers.

Here comes a truck

with garbage.

Here is a truck being loaded

with bread for the store.

Here comes the bread truck

They go over the bridge.

They come through tunnels.

here come the trucks.

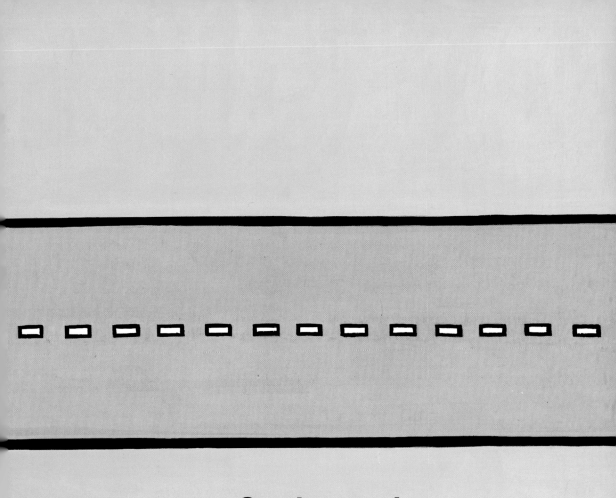

On the road

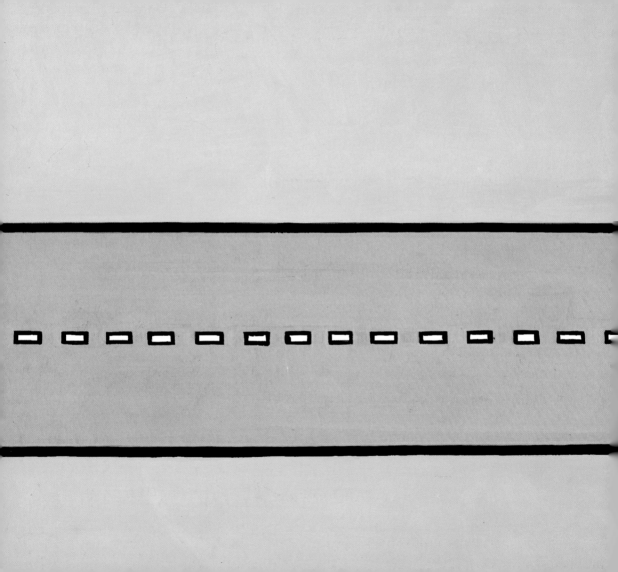

Trucks

Byron Barton

HarperCollins*Publishers*

Copyright © 1986 by Byron Barton. Manufactured in China. All rights reserved. For information address HarperCollins Children's Books, a division of HarperCollins Publishers, 195 Broadway, New York, NY 10007.
Library of Congress Cataloging-in-Publication Data   Barton, Byron. Trucks. Summary: Brief text and illustrations present a variety of trucks and what they do.   1. Trucks—Juvenile literature.
[1. Trucks]   I. Title.   TL230.B287   1986   388.3'24   [E]   85-47901   ISBN 0-694-00062-0
ISBN 0-690-04530-1 (lib. bdg.)
14 15 SCP 20 19 18 17 16 15 14 13 12